rec'd 11/09

MONSTER TRUCKS

by Kristin L. Nelson
photographs by David and Beverly Huntoon

Lerner Publications Company • Minneapolis

This book is available in two editions:
Library binding by Lerner Publications Company, a division of Lerner Publishing Group, Inc.
Soft cover by First Avenue Editions, an imprint of Lerner Publishing Group, Inc.
241 First Avenue North
Minneapolis, MN 55401 U.S.A.

Website address: www.lernerbooks.com

Library of Congress Cataloging-in-Publication Data

Nelson, Kristin L.
      Monster trucks / by Kristin L. Nelson; photographs by
David and Beverly Huntoon.
            p.   cm. — (Pull ahead books)
      Includes index.
      Summary: Introduces monster trucks and explains what
happens at a monster truck show.
      ISBN-13: 978-0-8225-0691-1 (lib. bdg. : alk. paper)
      ISBN-10: 0-8225-0691-2 (lib. bdg. : alk. paper)
      ISBN-13: 978-0-8225-0605-8 (pbk. : alk. paper)
      ISBN-10: 0-8225-0605-X (pbk. : alk. paper)
      1. Truck racing—Juvenile literature. 2. Monster trucks—
Juvenile literature. [1. Truck racing. 2. Monster trucks.
3. Trucks.] I. Title. II. Series.
GV1034.996 .N45 2003
796.7—dc21   2001006616

Manufactured in the United States of America
5 6 7 8 9 10 — JR — 12 11 10 09 08 07

What makes this truck different from other trucks?

This truck is a monster truck. Monster trucks fly through the air at monster-truck shows.

They crush cars.

Monster trucks race through mud.

They look big and mean—like monsters!

Monster trucks have giant tires. This
truck's tires are so big that you could
stand up inside them.

Monster truck tires have thick **tread**.
Tread helps the tires grip the dirt track,
so the truck does not slip.

A monster truck's giant tires are attached to its **frame**. The frame holds the tires and the **body** together. This monster truck has a red frame and a colorful body.

The driver rides high up in the body.
He sits in the cab.

Some monster trucks have special bodies. This tough truck has muscles!

Look at this truck. It is called Snake
Bite. Look at its body. How do you
think Snake Bite got its name?

VROOM, VROOM, VROOM! Monster trucks are louder than other trucks.

A monster truck has a very noisy **engine**.
An engine gives a monster truck power
and speed.

Monster trucks show off their power at monster-truck shows.

CRUNCH! This truck crushes cars
with its four big tires.

This truck glides high through the air.

This truck stands on its two back
wheels. It is doing a **wheelie**.

This truck races in a **mud-bogging** contest. The winner is the truck that goes farthest through thick mud.

These two monster trucks race around
a track.

The trucks go up a steep ramp during a race. Then they fly over a row of cars. Where do they land?

This truck lands on a ramp that slants toward the ground. Most monster trucks land safely on all four tires.

OUCH! This monster truck has rolled over. Is the driver safe?

Yes! Strong metal bars called a **roll cage** keep the driver from being crushed. The roll cage fits around the top of the cab.

Drivers wear seat belts and helmets for safety, too. When do you wear a seat belt or a helmet?

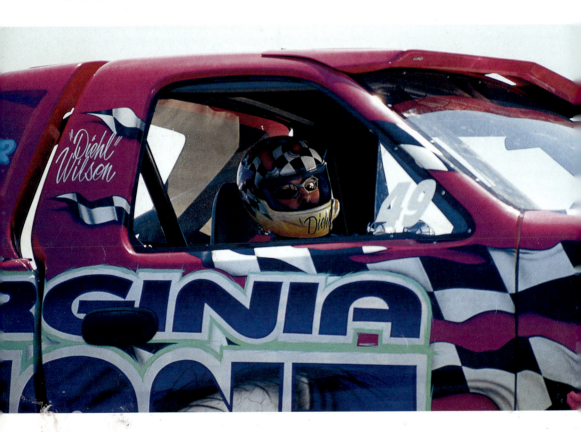

Look! This monster-truck driver has
finished his race safely. He is a winner!

Facts about Monster Trucks

■ There are two monster trucks that have extra huge tires. Their tires are 10 feet tall. That is as tall as a basketball hoop!

■ What would happen if a monster truck drove into a lake? Its giant tires have so much air inside them that the truck would float!

■ Some monster trucks have see-through floors. The drivers can see the tires and the track underneath them.

■ Most monster trucks do not have real headlights. Headlights are just painted on a monster truck's body. Real headlights are too heavy. They would slow down the truck.

Parts of a Monster Truck

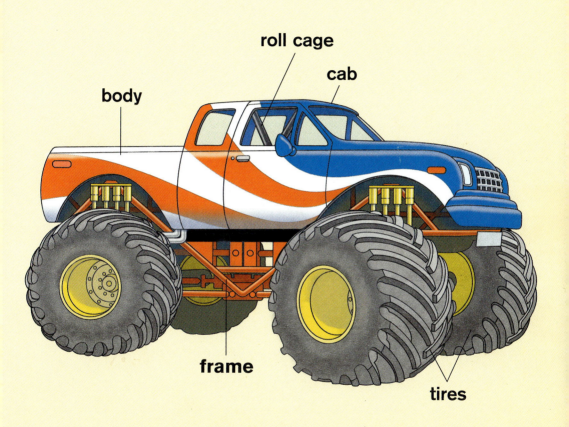

roll cage

cab

body

frame

tires

Glossary

body: the main part of a monster truck

engine: the part of a monster truck that gives it the power to move

frame: the part of a monster truck that holds together its main parts, such as the body, tires, and engine

mud-bogging: an event where two monster trucks race through thick mud

roll cage: bars that keep a monster-truck driver safe if the truck rolls over

tread: the raised parts of a tire that help it grip the ground and keep it from slipping

wheelie: a monster truck move. A monster truck stands on its two back wheels to do a wheelie.

Index

About the Author

Kristin L. Nelson loves writing books for children. Along with monster trucks, she has written about farm tractors and several animals for Lerner's Pull Ahead series. When she is not working on a book, Kristin enjoys reading, walking, and spending time with her son, Ethan, and husband, Bob. She and her family live in Savage, Minnesota.